INTRODUCTION

Humankind started fc
over 10,000 years agc
horizons and no light
rhythms of the heavens, and made connections
between the patterns in the night-sky and the
effects of the moon, planets, and stars on our
bodies, the oceans, and on our gardens.

Over the centuries as farming spread across
Europe, our ancestors determined the best times
to plant and harvest their crops, as well as for
animal husbandry, beekeeping, and timber felling.
This knowledge was handed down through the
generations in oral and written tradition.

With the development of chemical fertilisers in
the 20th century, these principles were forgotten
or ignored, but today we can still use this
knowledge to help our organic gardens flourish......

This is a short guide to the principles behind Lunar
Gardening. We show the major influences of the
moon and constellations to keep the calendar simple
and easy to interpret.

To find out more, visit www.LunarOrganics.com,
or refer to the more detailed **"Biodynamic Sowing
and Planting Calendar"** by Maria & Mattias Thun.

3

ABOUT BIODYNAMICS

Biodynamic growers believe that the farm should be managed as a single organism, self-sufficient in compost, manure, and animal feed, and as closely integrated with its environment as possible:

~ Biodynamic farms are diverse and a number of balanced crops are produced to ensure the whole ecosystem thrives.

~ Sprays and compost are made using organic waste and specific herbs. These are used, often in very small doses to improve the well-being of the soil, plants and animals.

~ Crops are planted and harvested in accordance with Lunar Gardening techniques to help connect the growth with the environment.

For the small-scale allotment holder, these principles are still valid. We may not be able to make our own preparations or keep our own farm animals, but we can keep our plots in balance with the environment. We can grow our produce organically, and use lunar gardening principles to help us.

You don't have to follow this approach blindly, so make your own observations. It's a time-tested approach with visible practical benefits, that helps to connect gardeners with the rhythms of nature !

LUNAR GARDENING PRINCIPLES

To take full advantage of the natural rhythms of the moon, we need to plan our activity in the garden by co-ordinating four things:

 1) MOON PHASE (p6)
   Is the moon waxing or waning ?

 2) MOON PATH (p8)
   Is the path across the sky
   ascending or descending ?

 3) MOON CONSTELLATION (p10)
   Which constellation is the moon
   passing in front of ?

 4) PLANT ASPECT (p11)
   What aspect of the plant needs to
   be stimulated ?

The lesser influences of the planets, and their geometric positions between each other and Earth are not shown on the calendar for clarity.

The calendar is colour-coded to show the different moon phases, paths, and constellations in each lunar cycle. You can choose the best days for various tasks by using the right colour combination.

An example for two days is shown on pages 18 &19

MOON PHASE

As the moon orbits the earth, it reflects sunlight.
Its position relative to the Earth and the Sun gives
rise to the different moon phases:

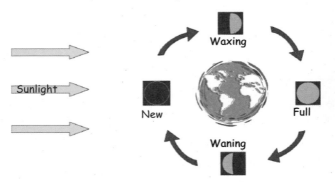

The moon orbits the earth in 27.3 days (the siderial month), but the earth is also moving round the
sun, so the moon phases seen from Earth follow a
Lunar Month of 29.5 days.   The waxing and waning
phases are the same in the Southern hemisphere,
but appear differently in the sky.

The lunar cycle has a major influence on the Earth
The tides are the most obvious manifestation, but
water table heights, the fluids in plants and the
soil, and reflected sunlight all play their part in how
we humans, as well as animals, and plants react to
the moon phases.

NEW MOON
At the start of the lunar cycle, the moon is between the Sun and Earth. It marks a change of direction in the moons' energies.

WAXING MOON:
When the moon is waxing, the soil is releasing, a bit like us exhaling breath. The growing energies are drawn into the **upper plant**. **Sow** plants that are grown for their properties **above ground** (everything except root vegetables) during the waxing moon.

FULL MOON
This too marks a change of direction of the moon's energies, like slack water between a rising and falling tide. Seeds germinate well just before full moon.

WANING MOON:
When the moon is waning, the soil is "inhaling" and **absorbing**. The growing energies are pulled down **towards the roots.** This is the time to **water,** or use **natural fertilizers** which are well absorbed by soil and into the plant. **Sow root crops** like carrots, beets, radishes, potatoes etc during a waning moon.

The moon phase is shown in the traditional way with a symbol in the top right corner of each day.

MOON PATH

The moon moves across the sky in a different path every night in a lunar month. The path ascends for 14 days and descends for 14 days. In effect it does in 27.3 days what the sun does in one year.

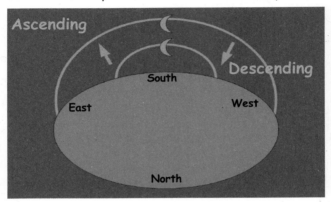

The moon path becomes more pronounced the nearer you are to the poles, and is barely apparent at the equator. Its influence on plants is also weaker at the equator.

Because the effect is caused by the moons orbit round the Earth, it is on a 27 day siderial month, and so does not coincide with the moon phase.

When the moon is ascending in the Northern hemisphere it is descending in the Southern hemisphere, just like summer and winter seasons.

Ascending Moon

The path starts at its lowest point in the sky, and each night for 2 weeks climbs a little higher. This makes it visible longer in the night sky. Moonrise and moonset move further towards the north.

The moon is passing in front of the constellations of Saggittarius, Capricorn, Aquarius, Pisces, Aries, Taurus, entering Gemini.

An **ASCENDING** moon path draws the sap of the plants upwards, which makes it a good time for **grafting**, and for **harvesting** any produce that grows above the ground.

 On the calendar an Ascending moon is shown as Light blue shading on the top of each day box.

Descending Moon

The path starts at its highest point in the sky, and each night for 2 weeks gets a little lower. This makes it visible for less in the night sky. Moonrise and moonset move further towards the south.

The moon is passing in front of the constellations of Gemini, Cancer, Leo, Virgo, Libra, Scorpio, entering Sagittarius.

A **DESCENDING** moon path draws the sap down so its a good time to **plant or transplant** seedlings. The roots connect a lot better with the soil helping the plant to establish itself faster

On the calendar a Descending moon is shown as dark blue shading on the top of each day box.

THE MOON AND CONSTELLATIONS

On the calendar, the Moons' path in front of each constellation is shown by reference to the colour shown for the day, and by the zodiac sign.

During the lunar cycle, the moon passes through 12 unequal sectors derived from the stellar constellations, (referenced by zodiac signs). The passage of the moon in front of each Constellation is based on **Astronomical data** and therefore differs from the traditional astrological division of equal 30 degree sections.

Each constellation is associated with one of **4 categories,** representing the **4 Elements (Air, Water, Fire and Earth)** and each Element enhances one particular aspect of each plant (see below).

PLANT ASPECT

On the calendar, the plant aspects are colour-coded, with illustrations as examples.

We use different parts of plants for different purposes, so it is important to understand which part (or aspect) of a plant we need to nurture, and the moon's effect on each aspect.
For example we grow Tomato plants for their fruits (rather their leaves, roots or flowers).
We grow carrots for their roots, spinach for the leaves and lavender for the flowers ˖

ROOTS are associated with Earth signs
Root days are shown in brown

FLOWERS are associated with Air signs
Flower days are shown in yellow

LEAVES are associated with Water signs
Leaf Days are shown in green

FRUIT are associated with Fire signs
Fruit days are shown in red

A lot of **vegetables** that grow above ground are classified as **fruit** (Eg: tomatoes, cucumber, courgettes, beans and peas, pumpkin, peppers) as well as 'obvious' fruits like strawberries, apples, pears, plums, cherries ....

The moon passes one of the Earth constellations:

♑ Capricorn

♉ Taurus

♍ Virgo

ROOT DAYS

For cultivating **Potatoes** and other **root crops** such as carrots, parsnip, onion, garlic, and radish choose **root days**

 Plant during the **descending lunar orbit**

 Sow on **rootdays**, preferably with a **waning moon** (because they are underground)

 Fertilize during a **waning moon,** for better absorbtion of the fertiliser

 Harvest and **store on root days** when the moon is **descending,** (because the crop is under ground). Alternatively harvest on root days with a waning moon

The moon passes one of the Air constellations:

 Gemini

 Libra

 Aquarius

FLOWER DAYS

Use" **flower days**" for cultivating **flowers**, **flowering herbs** (eg Camomile), **flowering hedges**, **flowering trees** (eg Lilac).

 Plant and prune whilst the moon is **descending**, ideally on yellow flower-days, when the sap is drawn to the roots

 Sow on **flowerdays**, preferably with a **waxing moon**

 Fertilize when the moon is **waning**, whilst the soil is absorbing.

 Graft, (roses) **store** (bulbs) or **harvest** (flowering herbs), on Flower days (yellow) when the **moon is ascending, and the sap is rising up**

The moon passes one of the Water constellations:

)(Pisces

M. Scorpio

69 Cancer

LEAF DAYS (GREEN)

Choose **leaf days** for salads, spinach, leaf herbs (mint, basil), leeks, cabbages and cauliflower as well as grass or non flowering hedges.

 Plant or prune (hedges) during a **descending moon** (sap is drawn to the roots).

 Sow leaf - plants on a **leafday**, preferably when the moon is **waxing**

 Fertilize when the moon is **waning,** (when the soil is inhaling) and ideally on a "leafday".

 Harvesting is normally best when the moon is **ascending**. However, to **store** your leaf harvest, **use fruit or flower days,** as the watery element present on leaf-days is NOT good for storing.

The moon passes one of the Fire Constellations:

 Aries

 Saggitarius

 Leo

FRUIT DAYS (RED)

Fruit Days are for all **fruits** (stawberries, rasberries, apples, plums)....as well as **all fruiting vegetables** like tomatoes, cucumber, courgettes, beans, peas, peppers, pumpkins....

 Plant or replant the seedlings, **Prune** fruit trees during a **descending moon** (sap is drawn down to the roots)

 Sow fruiting vegetables on **fruitdays**, preferably on a **waxing moon**

 Fertilize fruit plants and vegetables (tomatoes,cucumber..) **on a waning moon**, whilst the soil is inhaling and absorbing, ideally on **fruitdays**,

 Graft fruit trees/shrubs and **harvest** fruits and 'fruiting' vegetables **for storage** on an **ascending moon** (whilst the sap is rising, ideally **on fruit days**

MOON GARDENING METHODS

Taking cuttings
When taking cuttings, we want to preserve the
'cut' growth, so it is best to take cuttings/scions
when the moon is at the end of its ascending path.
We then plant the cuttings on a descending moon,
ideally on the right 'day' for the type of cutting
(eg Fire days for fruit, flower days for roses and
geraniums, leaf days for non-flowering shrubs).
Maria Thun has made a number of trials on this
subject.

Grafting
When grafting, we want the energies of the
'receiving' plant to be above ground, so we take the
graft on an ascending moon, and also transplant on
the ascending moon.

Pruning
With pruning, we want to remove excess growth,
so this is best done on a descending moon, because
the plant energy is then in the roots. This helps to
keep the pruned plant strong.

Cutting Grass
The same logic applies as pruning - The best time
is therefore on a descending moon, preferably on a
leaf day.

Weeds and weeding

Before you start getting rid of weeds (hopefully without weedkillers!), use them to your advantage. Many weeds contain important minerals which are used in herbal medicine, or can be used for mulching or liquid fertilisers (see page 26 for recipies). Some weeds prefer certain soils so they can also indicate what the soil is rich in.

When you need to get rid of them;
1) Use a 3-tyned tool to work the whole area on a day **when the Moon stands in Leo during a waxing moon in spring.** (Leo is always in a waxing moon in spring). This will encourage any weed seeds to germinate; the closer to full moon, the better.....
2) Hoe the area soon afterwards to remove the newly germinated weeds, **when the moon stands in Capricorn on a waning moon.** (Capricorn is always on a waning moon in spring).
3) IF you finish in autumn with the beds all hoed again on a **waning** moon, it leaves them well prepared for next season.

If the weather or your time won't allow the above, you could choose a different fruit day on a waxing moon, followed by another root day on a waning moon. Groundwork around plants should be done at the right time (eg. leaf veggies on leaf days).

USING THE CALENDAR

Pick the best days to do your gardening by matching th[e]
moon path and moon phase, and of course the weather

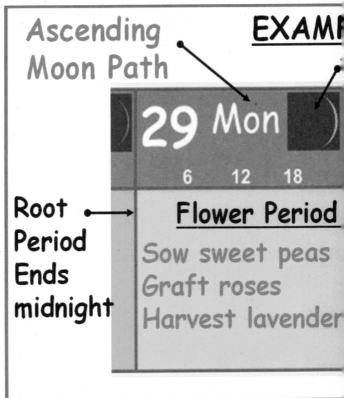

Ascending Moon Path

EXAMP[LE]

29 Mon

6   12   18

Root Period Ends midnight

Flower Period

Sow sweet peas
Graft roses
Harvest lavender

t aspect (colour) with the optimal lunar conditions of
 e season. The times are given as GMT.......

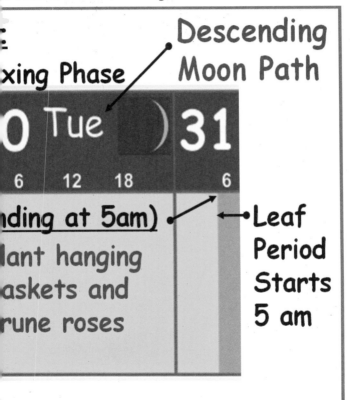

Descending
Moon Path

xing Phase

0 Tue 31

6   12   18   6

ding at 5am)

lant hanging
askets and
rune roses

•Leaf
Period
Starts
5 am

PLANNING YOUR ALLOTMENT

Some people like to grow their crops in orderly straight lines - Others (like me) prefer to lay out their crops more naturally and mix their crops with other plants or flowers that are mutually beneficial. You need to consider **crop rotation** (to keep your soil healthy) and **companion planting** (to allow different plants to help each other) as well.

In biodynamic gardening, it makes sense to grow the same groups (root, fruit, leaf and flower) together, as it's easier to hoe, and easier when working by dates from the calendar.

For example, grow courgettes together with corn, carrots with onions, cucumbers behind the corn for wind protection. Try different planting patterns (spirals, hearts, circles) just for fun!

Crop Rotation
Crop rotation ensures the nutrients in the soil do not become exhausted or disease-prone. If you have lots of room and use similar areas for each of your crops, you can rotate them. This method works commercially but, as an alternative, start with 'very demanding' plants (eg cabbages), then grow 'less greedy' plants (eg beans and beetroot) then grow 'light' plants (eg lettuce, peas, herbs). Ideally this would be followed by a 'fallow' period.

Companion Planting

Some plants support each other by deterring pests, providing shelter and a microclimate, or releasing nutrients. Marigolds (Tagetes) are particularly useful for detering nematodes. Another good example is to plant a few tomatoes between cabbages to deter caterpillars. The table on page 34 shows some common combinations of plants.

Raised Beds

These allow you to make your own soil mix, and of course need less stooping. Use old timbers (avoid 'creosoted' railway sleepers!) with stakes to hold them in place, then add your soil mix inside the frame. A good frame size is 2m x 1m x 30cm. (6ft x 3 ft x 1 ft), which allows you to walk round without walking on the soil. Try a thick layer of mulch in the summer, to keep everything moist.

Digging

You may have heard about no-dig, or even double-dig soil preparation. I personally try to preserve the soil 'structure' as much as possible (no dig), but sometimes deep-rooted weeds leave me no choice!

Whatever you choose, the soil has top priority, and needs to be managed carefully. Keep the soil moist by mulching regularly, and keep it aereated.

SOIL CONDITIONS

Most gardeners are aware that the soil is the foundation of the garden, and dictates how successful your plot will be.

Test the soil for pH and nutrients in order to add the right fertilisers. You can buy PH meters from any garden centre.

Acidic soil has a pH of less than 7
Alkaline soil has a pH of more than 7

Most vegetables prefer a slightly acidic soil.

The structure can vary from coarse sand to clay. To test it, take a hand-full of moist soil and squeeze it. Sandy soil will crumble through your fingers, and clay forms a hard ball. The best soil is of course somewhere in between, but changes take a while, so start by growing vegetables that favour your kind of soil.

Sandy soil
Sandy soil doesn't get waterlogged, is easily worked, and tends to be more acidic. You have to keep it covered with plants or mulch, or green manure to keep the water and nutrients available for the roots.

Carrots and radishes love sandy soils.

Clay soil

A clay soil has the advantage of holding nutrients better, and tends to be alkaline, but it's more difficult to work. It becomes easily compacted, is quickly waterlogged, and when dry it becomes hard and cracked, so it can't release nutrients to roots. Add lots of organic matter, encourage worms to do the digging for you, and add sand or, in extreme cases, small amounts of lime.

Composting

Compost your kitchen waste, with grass cuttings and garden waste to improve soil. If you have a compost heap, make sure it is on a sheltered position, protected from heavy rain and wind, and cover the heap with straw, or an old blanket. This prevents the heap getting too wet in heavy rain, or dry out in strong winds. The moisture content is important (neither too wet or too dry).

There are lots of different options on how to compost your waste, and choices of container. I use a simple 'open box', but plastic bins with holes also work well. Local councils often have free information and subsidised recycled plastic compost bins.

Biodynamic gardeners add special preparations to their compost (available from the BDAA) in order to get the best resullts.

PEST MANAGEMENT

We all hate them, but they do have a role in the ecosystem, so we need to manage their numbers by organic means. Here are a few suggestions:

SLUGS

Mild winters and wet summers (sound familiar?) can produce plagues of them:

a) Check all hiding places (under boards, in cracks in soil, under leaves, and other dank places. Rake your beds in Autumn.

b) During summer lure them into traps (beer in sunken cups) or create a shady place where they will hide in the day, and collect them.

c) Use sawdust, pine needles, or broken eggshells scattered at the base of plants to stop them (but this works best in dry weather when slugs are less of a problem).

d) You can also use copper rings round your plants, as this sets up an electrical reaction when the slug tries to cross it.

e) If you use raised beds you can buy a roll of coarse sandpaper from a builders merchant, and pin the sandpaper onto the wooden walls of the raised beds.

f) Bend a sheet of any metal to form an outward facing downward overhang they can't climb over.

g) Encourage wildlife (hedgehogs, birds, toads) to eat them.

Caterpillar

Plant a few tomatoes between your cabbages and brassicas, or mulch the rows between them with tomato leaves, as they hate the smell.

Make a tea of Alchemilla (wormwood) Tansy, or Tomato leaves (see page 26) and spray on the leaves. Repeat during the dangerous time in July and August.

Use netting and check leaves regularly both sides for eggs or catepillars)

Carrot fly

Best to avoid it by sowing carrots early. Do not use manure on your carrot bed, even in autumn, and choose a windy site if possible. Use tea made with onions and garlic, and cover with closhes. You can plant garlic, onions, leeks next to carrots or use strong-smelling herbs as mulch between rows.

Flea Beetles

These are mainly a problem on Mustard, Rocket, Radishes and Mizuma. Hoe regularly round the crop and keep moist with mulch, or cover with fleece. Spraying with Wormwood or Tansy (see page 26 for recipies) will also help.

GARDEN REMEDIES

Liquid Fertiliser:
Rich in nitrogen, so ideal for greedy feeders, such as Cabbages, leeks, tomatoes. DO NOT use on beans or peas).
Chop non-seeding weeds (eg nettles or comfrey) in pieces into a suitable container (waterbutt, plastic bin) and fill with rainwater. Leave in the sun with some airspace to allow for foaming, and add a net to prevent birds from drowning. Stir at least once per day. After 10 days the fermenting should be complete (and very smelly!). Dilute 1 part extract to 10 parts water before fertilising.

Anti-Fungal Preparation:
Horsetail Infusion:
Rich in Silicea. Used to prevent fungal diseases
Use fresh (about 500g) or dried (50g) horsetail and soak in about 3 litres of rainwater for 24 hrs. Bring to the boil and simmer for 15-20 minutes. Dilute up to 1:10 and spray on plants.
If the fungus has spread, then repeat for 3 consecutive days, or pour onto the soil to draw fungus back into soil

Anti-Bug Preparation
Tansy or Wormwood Infusion

Use fresh (100g) or dried (10g) Tansy or Wormwood as above, or use boiling water (no soaking required). Dilute up to 1:10.
Spray on plants to keep bugs off.

WATERING

Water is a valuable resource and should be used sparingly. In dry spells we are far too tempted to get the garden hose or sprinkler out, often when it is not needed. You can actually damage the plant by watering on a hot day with a sprinkler!

It is better to soak the base of the plant thoroughly (either early morning or late evening) once or twice per week, as this encourages the roots to grow deeply and stronger, drawing nutrients up to the plant.

Watering little and often (eg with a sprinkler) causes the roots to stay near the surface and become weaker and more vulnerable during a dry spell.

For some thirsty crops (such as tomatoes, cucumbers, courgettes and beans), a thick layer of mulch will keep them moist.

If you add anything to water for fertilising, choose a waning moon as this will help absorbtion by the soil.

<u>GROWING COMMON VEGETABLES</u>

The following examples show how to grow 4 common allotment produce. You can use them to look up similar 'types' of plant, or use the table inside the back cover for basic instructions.

Root Vegetable (page 29):   Potatoes

Flowers (page 30):   Sweet Peas

Leaf Vegetable (page 31):   Summer Salad

Fruit Vegetable (Page 32):   Tomato

For more detailed instructions and growing tips on specific common vegetables, please see our new Lunar Organics booklet:

Biodynamic Seed Guide

This gives lunar gardening instructions in a similar format to that shown opposite for all the most popular vegetables and is available from our website.
We can also supply these popular variants of biodynamic seeds from our online catalogue.

You can order online or pay by cheque at:

www.LunarOrganics.com

POTATOES

Plant

Root days on a waning or descending moon, mid March to mid May.
Place about 7cm deep in trenches or holes about 50 cm apart, with about 50cm between rows.

Fertilise

Waning Moon.
Beds best prepared in Autumn, or use well-rotted compost to fill trenches or holes. Keep moist when flowering.

Harvest

Root days on a descending moon for good storage, when leaves are yellow.

Tips   Use blight-resistant seed potatoes. Chit before planting by exposing seed potatoes to light (not direct sunlight) with eyes upwards. Use Horsetail (page 26) to counter fungal disease.

SWEET PEAS

Sow   Flower days with a Waxing Moon. Sow outside in March/April or earlier under glass. Sow 5cm deep, 2-3 seeds every 10 cm.

Plant   Flower days, descending moon, in spring with 30cm between rows, with support.

Fertilise   Flower days and a waning moon. Needs compost or mulch to keep moist.

Harvest   Flower days. Pick frequently to prevent seed formation, which stops further flowering.

Tips Soak seeds in warm water before sowing. Watch out for slugs.

SUMMER SALADS

Sow Leaf days, preferably a Waxing Moon from Feb/Mar under glass, or April to end-July outside.

Plant Leaf days, pref a descending moon, better in the evening or a shady day

Fertilise Doesn't need extra fertiliser Ensure soil has enough compost. Hoe on leaf days.

Harvest Harvest mornings for fresh consumption. For loose-leaf varieties, pick small leaves whenever you need them.

Tips When transplanting seedlings, clip longer roots and don't plant too deep. Keep soil moist, watch out for slugs, and hoe regularly. Don't plant next to parsley.

31

TOMATO

Sow		Fruit days with a Waxing Moon. Under glass Feb/March on. Best at 21 -24 deg.
Plant		Fruit days and a descending moon. They need support + sunny sheltered spot. Plant deep after last frost.
Fertilise		On fruit days and a waning moon. Needs plenty of compost or manure. Keep moist
Harvest		Ascending moon on Fruit days. Keep green tomatos on vine to ripen indoors, covered with a cloth.

Tips   Use mulch (comfrey or tomato leaves). Infusion of Horsetail is useful to prevent blight. Don't plant next to potatoes. Pinch tops off in Sept to stop growth.

IN SUMMARY

Plant, transplant and prune when the moon path is descending, preferably recognizing favourable root/flower/leaf and fruit days .

Harvest, store and graft when the moon path is Ascending. For storing(non-root)avoid LEAFDAYS.

Fertilize, water or applying anything to be absorbed by the soil during the waning moon.

Sow for plants above the ground when the moon is waxing, again recognizing the relevant days (leaf,fruit, flower). Sow rootcrops on a waning moon

Time for gardening is precious, and often has to be fitted round other commitments - if you can't pick and choose the optimal day, try to get the moon phase and path right or use alternatives.

Other influences, such as the season and the weather are more important. For example, harvesting Chamomile flowers on a wet and rainy day would not give good results, even if it's on a flower day whilst the moon is ascending!

Good luck and joy in your garden, - I would love to hear from your own experiments and comments .

Companion Planting Table	Beans (Climb)	Beans (Dwarf)	Beetroot	Cabbages	Carrots	Courgette	Cucumber	Garlic	Leeks	Lettuce	Onions	Peas	Potatoes	Sweetcorn	Swiss Chard	Tomatoes
Beans (Climb)				G		G	G	P	G	G	P	G			G	
Beans (Dwarf)			G				G		G	G	P	G	G	P		G
Beetroot		G		G	P	G	G	P	G		G		G	P	P	P
Cabbages	G	G	G				G		G	G	P	G			G	
Carrots			P					G	G	G	G	G	G			G
Courgette	G		G								P	G				G
Cucumber	G	G	G	G				P		G		G	P	G		G
Garlic	P		G	G	G		P			G			P			G
Leeks	P	G		G	G		P			G	G					
Lettuce	G	G	G	G	G		G	G	P			G			P	
Onions	P	P	G	P	G				P			G				
Peas	G	G		G	G		G		G	G	G			P	P	
Potatoes		G	P				P	P						G	P	
Sweetcorn		P				G	G			P		P	G			G
Swiss Chard	G			P	P	G										
Tomatoes		G	P	G	G	G	G	G	G	G	P	G		G	G	

■ = A good combination when planted together

▦ = A poor mix of plants - avoid if possible

☐ = A neutral combination of plants

Lunar Gardening examples for common plants

Plant	Aspect	Sow	Plant	Harvest
Apple Tree	Fruit		Descend	Ascend
Beans	Fruit	Waxing	Descend	Ascend
Beetroot	Root	Waning	Descend	Descend
Broccoli	Flower	Waxing	Descend	Ascend
Brussel Spr	Leaf	Waxing	Descend	Ascend
Cabbage	Leaf	Waxing	Descend	Descend
Carrots	Root	Waning		Ascend
Cucumber	Fruit	Waxing	Descend	Ascend
Garlic	Root		Descend	Descend
Leeks	Leaf	Waxing	Descend	Ascend
Lettuce	Leaf	Waxing	Descend	Ascend
Onion	Root	Waning	Descend	Descend
Parsnips	Root	Waning		Descend
Peas	Fruit	Waxing	Descend	Ascend
Peppers	Fruit	Waxing	Descend	Ascend
Potatoes	Root			Descend
Rosemary	Leaf	Waxing	Descend	Ascend
Roses	Flower		Descend	Ascend
Spinach	Leaf	Waxing		Ascend
Strawberry	Fruit		Descend	Ascend
Sweet Peas	Flower	Waxing	Descend	

QUICK REFERENCE

New   Waxing   Full   Waning

Ascending Moon   Descending Moon

Root   Fruit   Flower   Leaf

BEST DAYS

Activity:	GOOD	and/or	BEST
Sow (above grd):	Waxing	Ascend	Day
Sow (root crops):	Waning	Descend	Rootday
Plant:	Descend		Day
Prune:	Descend	Waning	Day
Graft:	Ascend	Waxing	Day
Fertilise:		Waning	Day
Water:	Waning		Day
Hoe:	Waning		Day
Harvest (non-root)	Ascend		Day
Harvest (root)	Descend		Rootday

LunarOrganics.com

ISBN: 978-0-9557767-1-7

ISBN 978-095577671-7

9 780955 776717

Published by Tidegraph Ltd

Booklet and calendar design © 2007 Tidegraph Ltd